charles Henri Ford

FLAG OF ECSTASY

selected poems

EDITED BY EDWARD B. GERMAIN

BLACK SPARROW PRESS LOS ANGELES
1972

The cover photograph of Charles Henri Ford is by Henri Cartier-Bresson (Paris, 1935).

Acknowledgements are due to the editors of the following periodicals where some of these poems first appeared: *Blues, Caravel, Compass, Diogenes, Fantasy, Furioso, London Bulletin, New Directions, Poetry* (Chicago), *Poetry World, The Harvard Advocate, The Tiger's Eye, The Virginia Spectator, Transition, View, VVV*. The editor acknowledges the assistance of the libraries at the University of Michigan, the University of California at Los Angeles, and the University of Texas at Austin where Charles Henri Ford's Archives are housed.

SBN 87685-100-6 (paper edition)
SBN 87685-101-4 (signed cloth edition)

Black Sparrow Press
P.O. Box 25603
Los Angeles, California
90025

9/77- Bleiwiss-# 1815

Also by Charles Henri Ford

Prose (with Parker Tyler)

The Young and Evil (1933)

Poetry

A Pamphlet of Sonnets (1936)
The Garden of Disorder (1938)
ABC's (1940)
The Overturned Lake (1941)
Poems for Painters (1945)
The Half-Thoughts, The Distances of Pain (1947)
Sleep in a Nest of Flames (1949)
Spare Parts (1966)
Silver Flower Coo (1968)

TO

A. EVERETT AUSTIN, JR.
CHRISTIAN BERARD
ANDRE BRETON
GERTRUDE CATO
JEAN COCTEAU
CARESSE CROSBY
E. E. CUMMINGS
ISAK DINESEN
MARCEL DUCHAMP
BILLIE HOLIDAY
EUGENE JOLAS
MARIE LAURE
MARIE MENKEN
ZACHARY SCOTT
EDITH SITWELL
GERTRUDE STEIN
FLORINE STETTHEIMER
PAVEL TCHELITCHEW
CARL VAN VECHTEN
PETER WATSON
WILLIAM CARLOS WILLIAMS
STARK YOUNG

INTRODUCTION

In his archives at the University of Texas, there is an exchange of letters between Charles Henri Ford and John Crowe Ransom concerning Ford's poem "The Overturned Lake." Ransom refused to publish it in the *Kenyon Review*. "Where you are clear," he wrote, "you don't seem distinguished. But when you sound distinguished, you are not (to me) clear. . . . I think you have a lot of stuff, and that your strategy is bad. . . . In part, your technique is not developed. . . . You are the logical end to which modern tendencies come, I am sure of that."

In one form or another, charges like these were made against *all* the early surrealists, in every country: their poetry was not intellectual enough, too arbitrary, redundantly Freudian, and obscure. Occasionally these criticisms are spoken today: "I'll tell you why surrealism died," one aging academic critic said to me, "we just couldn't understand it."

Surrealism has not died, it has grown. Charles Henri Ford published his first surrealist poem in 1929; for forty years thereafter, surrealism thrived in the avant-garde, beyond academia and established tradition. Gradually, it has transformed the shape of modern poetry and become an influence of major proportions. In an oblique way Ransom's comment to Ford was prophetic, "You are the logical end to which modern tendencies come . . . . " But the charge of obscurantism was inaccurate.

"The Overturned Lake," for example, is a poem about the unconscious mind. It begins with a lake, surrounded by mountains. There is a tunnel where a train rumbles. A bus worms along the mountain road. The vibrations of the passing vehicle ripple the lake.

Beside it sits the poet, trying to understand what he cannot see; the depths of the lake, the depths of his own mind. He hears the "blue unsolid tongue" of the lake lap the shore in unintelligible noises. "Tongue of a deafmute" he calls it, and exclaims, "I am concerned in your overthrow":

> *I should like to pick you up, as if you were a*
> *woman of water,*
> *hold you against the light and see your veins flow*

7

with fishes; reveal the animal-flowers that rise
nightlike beneath your eyes.

The poem moves from metaphors through symbols to the surreal. At the beginning a fanciful conceit compares the landscape to an enormous head — the mountains are its brain, the lake its tongue. Then Ford treats the lake symbolically: "You are like the mind of a man, too." And the train becomes a symbol of modern incursions into the unconscious, which for centuries had remained as unviolated as a remote mountain lake.

Gradually, the poet "turns" the lake into a strange kind of poem, "as unpredictable as the human body," where veins flow with fishes and carnal flowers bloom in its dark like fears. The last lines transform the unconscious water into the water of the unconscious, filling it with the energy of dreams. There, the poet watches desire rising noiselessly in a memory, sees it surface to upset the calm of the conscious mind and to make the heart turn over with dread.

A passage in one of Ford's notebooks bears on the creative activity behind this poem. It records his astonishment at Jung's statement that bodies of water are frequently used as symbols of the unconscious. "Could I possibly have had this in mind when I wrote 'The Overturned Lake'?" he asks.

In other words, "The Overturned Lake" was written, at least in part, by his unconscious mind. It may not have been entirely "automatic," but even with such obvious phrases as "blue-unconscious bed," Ford does not seem to have been aware of the significance of the symbols that rose into his mind: the poem's general meaning comes from an area not subject to his conscious scrutiny.

"This yielding to the Unconscious," writes Edith Sitwell in her preface to Ford's third book of poetry, "is at the root of surrealism." It is the source of its astonishing power, and a primary reason for its influence and longevity. Submitting to the unconscious gives images dream potency; Ford isolates this power in the short poem on page 108. It also gives poems dream structures, organizing them not by intellectualizations, but by patterns of desire. It changes the way one reads the poetry. William Carlos

8

Williams, in his introduction to Ford's first book of poetry, *The Garden of Disorder*, speaks of "a special condition of the mind" that this poetry generates "which to me seems the gist of the poems, and the only way to understand them."

Another World War was beginning as that volume of poetry was published. Other poets wrote about the war, but Ford's work, and American surrealism in general, was a "counterfoil." Williams writes: "This sort of particularly hard, generally dream-like poetry is inevitable today when the practice of art tends to be seduced by politics." Ford's "world to which the usual mind is unfamiliar [is] in active denial of all the unformed intermediate worlds in which we live."

"There is no end of intermediates," Wallace Stevens comments elsewhere with surprising continuity, "but to be master of disorder requires so very much more than to be the master of order — and among other things the hilarity that Mr. Ford appears to possess."

Ford's first book welds together radio jazz and iambic pentameter, surrealist imagery and the sonnet form. It is American surrealism — it doesn't read like translations from the French — American in its hilarity and ingenuousness and its fascination with sex and slang and the lyrics of popular songs. In 1929, Ford called his first magazine *Blues* and his poetry is full of kinky jazz blues,

> *I must say your deportment took a hunk*
> *out of my peach of a heart.*
> *I ain't insured against torpedoes!*
> *My turpentine tears would fill a drugstore*

and witty satires of popular lyrics:

> *And the lasso of love has the ghost of a chance . . .*

Ford has composed varieties of poetry. He had an early interest in creating a surreal conceit, one whole step beyond metaphysical conceit. Several appear in his second book, *The Overturned Lake*, poems like "Narcissus in Winter," "Morning, Noon

9

and Night," or the title poem. He has written surrealist ballads, and short lyrics, even epigrams, both charming and bawdy:

> *Life, let me get you down I love you.*

Ford excels at the humorous *amour*, "Somebody's Gone," for example, or "I Wouldn't Put It Past You." His wit transforms "There's No Place To Sleep In This Bed, Tanguy" into a brilliant, hilarious tour de force that caricatures as it transcribes Tanguy's paintings. Frequently, this wit is erotic, as in "He Cut His Finger On Eternity" where Ford takes liberties with Whitman's homosexuality. This eroticism underlies some of his most original lyrics.

But his forte is the surreal image. He can write astonishing first lines:

> *I believe in the day hung between your hands,*

breathtaking endings:

> *leaving the body desolate as a staircase.*

In between, he creates miraculous images. The reader will find them.

If the problem of the realist poet is to show that the sky is *blue*, then the surrealist's is to show that the sky is colored by desire. Poems like "The Bad Habit" *embody* desire. "The Overturned Lake" shows ti influencing perception to overturn the phenomenal world. Ford can do all this in a single line:

> *Baby's in jail; the animal day plays alone . . .*

And it is neither preposterous nor obscure to realize that Baby, looking from his playpen, conceives everything in his own image, small unfurry animal. "Animal day" is reality easily transformed in the smallest eyes of desire.

No American poet before Ford has come up with so many extraordinary juxtapositions, and few have employed these images with such dexterity. No "reasonable logic" or daylight barrier seems to stop him. In one poem he changes the day from a free, autonomous poem into a horse. He turns the sky into an arm, a mouth, a man, a thief, and then into an enormous face. The sun, he makes into a wound, a jewel, an equation, an eye, a tear. Night is a ditch. All in eight lines, with obvious ease, and clarity.

Each poet has his few best poems, but the ones that are marred by a falling off in energy, or by a weak passage or a tediousness that sets in, may still contain something of the spirit of the poet that the more fully formed poems fail to catch. I think this is true in a few of Ford's longer poems; because of his genius for imagery, their parts can be greater than the whole. Edith Sitwell was especially fond of A through K, V, W, and Y in *ABC's*. "K is really extraordinary," she wrote him, "I congratulate you on the book."

When he began publishing in 1929, Ford was unique: America's surrealist poet. In retrospect, he is seminal. What he accomplished in 1930, most American poets hadn't even imagined. In the pages of his magazines, *Blues* and *View*, he introduced and encouraged surrealism while it passed into the spirit of hundreds of American writers. In his own work he creates the wonder, the wit, and the erotic beauty that have made surrealism the most significant of all modern influences upon poetry.

Edward B. Germain
Pomona College
February, 1972

TABLE OF CONTENTS

THE GARDEN OF DISORDER

The Garden of Disorder

to Pavel Tchelitchew

I

To lodge your harvest in the lion's mouth,
to telescope the bugs that feed flowers,
to place your aspiration under the microscope,
and send no disease to graze in the meadow of hours;
to bisect the raindrop, quarrel with snow,
contradict those who know;
to dig for the root of evil, lasso the worm,
pin the two-horned butterfly to the schoolbook,
fertilize the crook, the thief,
and others who till grief;
catalog the good postmaster
and those who hobble after
the plough of Christianity, or vanity;

to gauge the flight of reason
according to the fuel of unreason;
experiment with the chemicals, music and love,
and not leave the weather to the weather-man;
behoove the right to responsibility's ghost to
hoist the sheet at night;
to return the stare of houses
and of the beast that browses
this side of delirium,
among the meek displeased cattle
of Newark or Seattle;
to despise, despise nothing
but the mote of shame in your eye;

if the hunchback hinders the corn's turning yellow
the hump on his neck will not wither,
neither will the fellow
who eats the idiot's dinner
grow idiotic, or thinner:
he will reverence the monster

as well as the paragon blade
of grass that God made: though He will make another,
freaks are not mothers, even to freaks:
the vine that shrieks is normality's:
banality's blister may be pricked after twilight;

to curtail the snail were not heroic,
to become a stoic were to risk the seasons,
and so you may launch like five fishes
your five senses in aquatic regions
of the mind; though the octopus grow unacrobatic,
hearts will curl in competition;
as long as deeds throw shadows,
as long as shadows alter deeds,
as long as roots drink so the raw head may bleed:
resolve to recapture the machinery
of odors, the private rainbows, the leafless motors,
nor dread the drums of drought,
tear-gas of the sensational nor the
reactionary apple in the garden of the irrational.

II

Let us try dividing the impersonal, and personal,
imagination's cloak makes us invisible,
and spy unseen upon the habitation
of deities themselves unseen.
When the desert rearranges the sand's abstractions,
is one god seized with the frenzy of design
for pattern's range, or the madness of mutation —
to change a second god's creation?
Does the complex fountain roar,
and flay the simple air without a purpose,
or is it Peace lashed against War?
Who is there, who is there to say if the sun
fakes indifference to the flock it shines upon?

When hail beats, loudest of grain,
and water-holes retreat, maybe it is for fauns
that the earth yawns all of a sudden,
or is it the speechless snake
that causes the ground to gape?
If after nightfall the laurel staggers,
who reels more at sun-up than the tigers?

Do mountains rise up in wrath,
know what ills, if the wind
walks off with a hill's head — who is dead?
What is the language of minerals,
of emeralds what green feeling?
Is winter's stealing cursed by birch or birchwood,
does the thicket yearn? The rainbow ravishes
which rock, what cliff that the sea-water spangles?

Is the swart oak Othello who strangles
Desdemona, the forest-bride?
Oh, hide, hide, wildflower, tree-tower and bush,
you will be crushed by the war-storm's thumb!
Wherefrom the vengeance, how called the crime,
of myrtleberry and columbine?

When the trees ride bicycles,
do their haunches hear how they are headed, whence going,
or is the Brute's breath merely blowing,
blowing? Who can perceive
the sound of seaweed —
the same tympanum that records the mood
when the clouds stammer?
Whose the audition when the will is betrayed?
Oh why are we afraid? For Beowulf bellows
across the centuries to bravery's bedfellows.

III

Perfume the clock, and the cricket will take care of Aunt Bess,
but the poet forgot to put on his odor-proof vest:
how staunch the scent of words?
Dilute the sadistic monopoly's
whirlpool that twisted
the artist out of all recognition:
he will trail the secret brook
that runs with the fragrance of perdition.

But closet the coat-of-arms: why should the Worker's hands
build castles of quicksands: the dragon's firestream
rots not the dragon, the poppy is not oppressed
with the opium-dream.

You might deodorize the bat,
yet aeroplanes are not aghast at the night:
redolent are the boar and nettle,
though naught reeks of war save the fetid battle.
Inhale the constellations
and you may find them appetizing,
but mobilize the nation,
and whose gastronomy is it?

The cowboy's lariat
dips high for the lowest sweet chariot;
dawn will not break painlessly over the blindman's pate;
the lilies will be perpendicular
to the actress dying of cancer.
The fiddle cannot sprout legs
on the war-veteran who begs,
nor will all God's chillun get shoes
by hy-dee-hy-dee-hoing the blues.
Maybe the laburnum just grows, but if I were foreman,
I'd rather be the shepherd
who traded spoors with the leopard.

IV

Lenin has withdrawn to a dialectic
paradise and counts with sociological eyes
the biffs of the nightsticks, the devil's police.
No witch flies out of the window
in witchless New England;
oh the goblins sleep . . .
But how many roofs besides my own
leak with remorse
at liberty's affliction,
be the rain fine or coarse?

Mutable the oracle of the gloom that links night to day;
of the fat which attacks decay,
and the fit that enfolds the prophet;
of creation who loves those who create,
and death who dotes on masturbation;
of her lover in the asylum,
and your love on the lookout for a maniac;
of his morality on the right track,
and their abnormality on the wrong island;
and of any other wizard reason
to convict you of subjective treason,
a traitor to the snow-gardens and the equator,
to the zodiac masses, the classless solution
in May's revolving botany: bouquets of terror
from the garden of revolution.

The Jeweled Bat

for Djuna Barnes

It is with terror that the jeweled bat
at noon must flap the wavy air: night's sorrows
and morning's hate compel its cries to spat-
ter with thin blood the caverns and the hollows
that darkness in the body holds: entan-
gled in a sun it cannot see, escape
it finds to be the love promised to man
by angels: madness; heaven overripe.
So glory, automatic, probable,
reveals the hidden corpse of the mammal,
thus adding to death's momentary glut,
yet harboring the acrid obdurate salt
the lovely black bat used to fly across
not knowing then the solitude that was.

Fatigue

for Pavel Tchelitchew

Fatigue sits in the breast like a spring hare,
gnawing the gross red cabbage of your heart,
until entreated by the spurious dark
to jump into the room and be trapped there.
The murdered roots of a young vegetable,
like beauty frighted once, must wait upon
the fever of the earth from the hot sun,
to grow again into Cain's brother, Abel.
In my town after midnight there are no
dance-halls, doctors, or police of the soul,
in my room never a carpet of grass and gold
flowers. The rabbit leaping to and fro
would like to pay back Love, who keeps the only
whore-house where the cold wind jangles for money.

Unhappy Train

for Djuna Barnes

I have an infant with legs full of sores:
its mother is a girl whose life you know,
her fingernails are livid, her hair snow-
white; dolls dressed like the virgin or like whores
fly in and out the branches of a tree
inside her head, from which your father hangs
hearing unholy prayers or pious slang
the Magdalenes and Marys make for me.
My child and I ride this unhappy train:
it lies along the hard arms of its mother
across the aisle in your seat, in another
I must attend the rock's night-time, though fain
to speak my part in daylight and embrace
the baby before darkness grabs its face.

Dissatisfaction With Life

Your son is paralyzed:
look both ways through his eyes;
your daughter is silent:
go and live on another island
where waterfalls harden and slowly explode
like the lovers I connote,
inhabitants of a movie theatre,
deep-sea animals without water
or the trembling of a train
to wind the brain
or snowflakes or tears to drop
until someone says stop
save my life, haggard hours,
you will not save yours
by getting off at Sportland
and having your soul arrested.

The Desire To Be In Two Places At Once

Stones watch the sea like cats: the stone of sleep
pulls me away from the dream that creeps
like a cat to the shore: there hops the fish,
I; stone and cat: both mine to wonder at.

Stony sleep, smooth as fur, take away time.
Your twin scours the hills of dreaming, goes hungry,
    howls
back to the block whose paws are scarey,
there finds the fish whose hair is streaming,
probable food, and the snoring rock.

Sea's disharmony, a flying fish, waits cat-like,
flies rock-like straight to the cat's yawn,
whose fur hardens, washed by the paw of sleeping.
Rocks, now wide-awake cats, eye the cripple fishes:
each two wings, two wishes.

Undersea Disturbance On Times Square

The whales of longing flung themselves ashore
on the jagged rocks of the five-and-ten-cent store;
schoolboys fishing in the street of the undefined
heard the great jets spouting among the valentines
with a sigh like traffic, a noise like fear:
what phosphorescent power threw them there?
Whales as susceptible as little girls
wallowed on the counter strewn with false pearls;
schoolboys fishing in the furtive air of reason
reported the occurrence all in due season;
but one of them had dared put desire on his hook,
he cast his line with a pitiful look.
Scientists who studied the mass suicide
dislodged one youngster from a whale's inside.

Plaint

Before A Mob Of 10,000 At Owensboro, Ky.

I, Rainey Betha, 22,
from the top-branch of race-hatred look at you.
My limbs are bound, though boundless the bright sun
like my bright blood which had to run
into the orchard that excluded me:
now I climb death's tree.

The pruning-hooks of many mouths
cut the black-leaved boughs.
The robins of my eyes hover where
sixteen leaves fall that were a prayer:
sixteen mouths are open wide;
the minutes like black cherries
drop from my shady side.

Oh, who is the forester must tend such a tree, Lord?
Do angels pick the cherry-blood of folk like me, Lord?

THE OVERTURNED LAKE

Comedy Of Belief

I believe in the day hung between your hands:
shall I bridle the eggs of the evening,
or break them on the backs of boys,
or strengthen my night with a thong of shells?

I believe in your heart, that stray cat
who roams your body, looking for a home:
if I masked my face with its sparkling fur,
then would its eyes go out like lights?

I throw you the ball of the sea. Catch it.
I unroll a cloud, but we may fall through it.
I send you my legs, as if you were wingless.
You are the playmate I did not know had been planted.

Look with me at music: shadows of the soul;
listen to the sun, a prisoner that sings.
Believe with me that leaves have nothing to lock from
    you.
I believe that stars starve at the sight of you.

Oh let us take time by the hand, child of no one,
who grows up to look like everyone's son!
Do you wonder that the rain wires the hill with
    its hair?
Perhaps you take for granted all the mushrooms of
    memory?

When I show you the hours that have no father or
    mother,
I want to know if your mouth is more errant than
    an apple.
You have been in my boat when it staggered with
    melancholy:
what language's love-potion will veer me a lull?

Pianoplayer whose notes are wild honey,
the bears of my biography rub, rob your keyboard.

Why, the standstill room grows wobbly as a wood,
and the guardians of museums cry resurrection!

To tone down language is to tongue-tie the pulse,
meter of mood, tape-line of longing,
and so we are boosted by the measureless dream
and awake to an algebra whose symbols cry havoc.

Belief, mysterious as heat, and doubt,
twin apparitions, jerk my head about.
Doubt, you are cold as an ocean grave.
Belief, wary as any root, how much have I saved?

I believe in the curtain that rocks on nothing,
shall I tackle a corner: watch it race up my sleeve!
— or undrape a statue which isn't there at noon,
unless you will agree to change to marble at eleven.

Have I forgotten my pencil on your more than shelf?
Then I shall be sure to return, return
and fumble, like a savage with a bleak mechanism,
at the propped torso, the universal totem.

I toss you the brink of unhappiness: look over
and see how the clear veins of happiness flow;
then trigger these clumps in that gun of tunes
where brains are unneeded to say rat-a-tat-tat to.

Look around at the sick: do none of them resemble me;
question the healthy: would I have replied likewise?
Believe in the water-bright moon, eye of the rock-
     dark sea,
and as long as you lower your hand, the sunken sun
     will rise.

Let us inject this instant with the serum of death:
immortality's experiment! Each and every microbe

is just another sweetheart in love's laboratory.
What's the name of that virus you wanted me to worry?

When I walk out the door, the roof clamping my skull,
say, whose bed dangles on the hundred and nineteenth floor?
There are those who haul the familiar until it becomes strange,
therefore harness the new, or the horse will wagon you.

When sensation turns clown and our fright turns sawdust
and the buzz in our bones does a head-over-heels:
it's nonsense, with automatic grace, who goes round,
is tripped, gets up, and again falls down.

Ah beautiful obscurity, with the K.O. kiss!
When the operation's over you'll be oh so hulled:
gape now at the algebra whose symbols cry havoc;
the flower's afire though the spine of it chills.

Belief, mysterious as heat, and doubt,
twin apparitions, do they churn your ribs about?
Doubt! You are cold as an ocean grave.
Belief, uncertain engine, how much have you saved?

I believe in the third day, the first time, the last call;
in the orange with the seed of a peach and a plum's skin.
I conjure my balance as long as I know you are there,
but move and the map moves and my bearings give in.

I believe — but tell me what you believe and if you trust me
when I twist all the world's roads into a rope
and clamber to a blue planet, blossom of space,
only to discover that I've but gone around the block.

I catch the bell's ring of your voice's bone,
translate it as though it were the rind of intuition
left sprawling on the sidewalk by a child of three.
Now I slide back down the rope as if the cops were
     after me.

Look, quick, there goes the man born with his heart loose-
    hanging,
and here comes the one-legged lady with the false eyelashes;
if you find anyone who seems to know nothing and every-
    thing,
send him to me — I want to trade places — he's not crazy.

He tousles his reason as if it were someone's hair —
hey watch the fishes, phosphorous, faint and fall:
each illuminates a spot no bigger than a word;
let's set a trap of water and cage his airy verse!

When he puts his arms behind him and says, Which one?
: the left hand holds nothing and the right less than the dust.
Do you know what he means? Then choose! But think
of all that once was nothing and the dust that was every-
    thing.

The earth is a thrown stone, fruitful, flying.
Who threw it? Where will it rest?
Somebody's calling, Look out you'll get hit!
The heart, too, hurtles, and whatever we want goes with it.

While eggs bulge, music burns, stars say hello,
apples stagger, pulses rip, the dream pops open,
curtains harden, moons dissolve, love lasts often,
leaves unlock, age clowns, death and the lunatic listen, —

belief, mysterious as heat, and doubt,
twin apparitions, fold us both about.
Doubt will topple the last door, the cold grave's.
Belief, let the wind walk over us, and the grass wave.

"Baby's in jail; the animal day plays alone"

Baby's in jail; the animal day plays alone,
tame as the animal baby behind the bars of the crib:
the cub whose nose has not yet dipped
in the reek of excitation,
whose claws have not unbound the hide of habit,
nor scratched at pride, the skin,
and tasted sensation's blood.
Baby will come to grief and love.
Visitors to the family zoo
do not go to see a vegetarian tiger.

If the clover's leaves are four,
good luck's just behind the door.
If your hand goes through a mirror:
the glass is dear, but bad luck's dearer.
Swipe a horsehair from his tail, drown it in a waterpail:
it takes thirty days to make
horsehair turn into a snake.
You want a new dress, I do too.
You bite a butterfly, I'll chew a leaf.
Baby will come to love and grief.

"One day, one day"

One day, one day
calls the other days away.

Not as the dog of morning
trees the cat of afternoon;

but as watching time in a well
sink with its arms around the moon.

One moon, one face,
to other suns and jaws give place.

The Bad Habit

for Poe

Drug of the incomprehensible
engenders the freaks of desire.
The bleeding statue, the violin's hair,
the river of fire:

the blood grows, the hair flows, the river groans,
from the veins, from the skin, by the home of the child
pulled and repelled by Bloody Bones;
renewal of the swoon

mastered, the raw egg of fear,
doped with mystery, the hooded heart:
perpetually haunted, hopeless addict,
herding unheard of cattle!

Rider on the bat-winged horse.

"January wraps up the wound of his arm"

January wraps up the wound of his arm,
January, thieving as a boy, hides the jewel,
sunset, bright bleeding equation.

Day has written itself out, a giveaway, a poem
that balks like a horse before the ditch of night.

Tomorrow, the gash will be an eye:
a drop of dew will travel up his cheek,
like a tear that has changed its mind.

The Living Corpse

If I should build a fire in mid-air,
it would cast on the meadow a bird's trace,
but the flame would be less bright than your face,
the shadow less dark than your hair.

The fog hurries when the wind drives,
and the blackskinned trees return,
as you do, living corpse,
talking without a sound,
harmless and harmful as a sweet obsession;
I handle you as if I had found
a mermaid, or a plasmosome.

How warm you are to my arms,
how cold to all conduct!

The shroud of days cannot cover;
the knife of the night cuts through
memory's mist. You, bare as the sky,
refuse my heart's food,
yet refuse to die.

But I shall make a fire in mid-air,
to cast on my meadow a bird's trace,
and the flame will be less bright than your face
the shadow less dark than your hair.

A Fool To Do It

What drives you crazy?
All of anything, half of nothing:
the eye that drips, the head of hair,
the full meaning, the empty hour's stocking?

Who is that standing there?
The traces of insanity, how many to a pound:
the cut letter, the mangled thread,
the beaten track, the belt unbound,

the piano under the bed? I am a fool to believe it:
the forced food, or laugh, the tough weather;
the arbitrary reason; the fine, or breaking, point;
the turn in the other direction.

And so are you, lovely goat!
Pin these garlands of rage
around your throat: the picked up pieces.
Leap, now, from the page.

Winter Solstice

The leaf scraped of energy is veined
to formulate a branch, the seismograph
tuned to waves modeled like a long sigh.
Water, stunned by degrees, stops in its flight,
a cold bird counts three, then fades like a flame:
the charred remains of summer's delayed dead.
The tongue's a rapid leaf, any old man
may mock a chrysalis with butterfly words
until the secret of the rose is out —
that day the root will vow the sun forgot,
meaning and sound will drug his head like wine
and the dead limb decide for the live bird.
But the season's tongue continues to stop and start,
thawed and frozen, like the cold and hot heart.

Night Spent

Axe-train shook me from sleep,
sleep like blood on rooster feathers;
faucet turned till wrung neck dried,
sleep washed off like specks of lie.

Truth-train signalled by mind's bonfire;
Engineer Sleep ran roughshod o'er
thought-smokey heap on bedroom floor.

Axe shook brain;
you washed feathers
of my head; truth is you:
train is bed:
poem the bonfire we shot through.

Somebody's Gone

There may be a basement to the Atlantic
but there's no top storey
to my mountain of missing you.

I must say your deportment took a hunk
out of my peach of a heart.
I ain't insured against torpedoes!
My turpentine tears would fill a drugstore.

May I be blindfolded before you come my way again
if you're going to leave dry land like an amphibian;
I took you for some kind of ambrosial bird
with no thought of acoustics.

Maybe it's too late to blindfold me ever:
I'm just a blotter crisscrossed with the ink
of words that remind me of you.

Bareheaded aircastle,
you were as beautiful as a broom made of flesh and hair.

When you first disappeared
I couldn't keep up with my breakneck grief,
and now I know how grief can run away with the mind,
leaving the body desolate as a staircase.

Song

Eyes obsessed with blues
tone the zinc skin of the wild goose,

waif of the yellowy xylophone
I woo you as a wick the candle-bone.

Quick as the nick of vacant time
(thunder whittled to the marrow's rhyme)

this is a jingle for your jaw,
pearl-planted, a rant for the blest hee-haw

of the pink bee storing in your brain's
veins a gee-gaw honey for the golden skillet

set to heat on my heart's rubies
BABY WITH REVOLVER HOLDS HURRICANE AT
    BAY

Morning, Noon and Night

If you used for a fin
the hand hanging from your shoulder,
what ocean would you beg in
or swim harder
past the lace curtains turned to coral?

If I had my way you'd be a starfish
and no landlady would stand in the hall
then, and that man in room 4
would not play checkers all night and keep you awake:
he'd be a hermitcrab and move his shell miles

off, so you wouldn't be afraid to make
noise because you limp,
not because the lining of your coat
is ripped with refusals.

I am interested in your working conditions:
would they be better under water?
I've never noticed if you have a cushion
between you and the sidewalk, or ambitions.

You have only three fingers though,
morning, noon and night,
on your left hand, five on your right
hand hanging sorrowfully.

He Cut His Finger On Eternity

a poem for Walt Whitman

What grouchy war-tanks intend to shred
or crouch the road's middle to stop my copy?
I'll ride roughshod as an anniversary
down the great coiled gap of your ear.

And if I encounter hitchhiking inspiration
I'll give him a lift, we'll gallop double,
and the trees will invent new contortions to greet us
and the cats blink boldly, unhiding themselves.

Like libertines we'll plunge frontiers
romantic as a journey, unromantic as a slum,
wrap up with a river for a spy's disguise,
and wig you with time, the waterfall.

Who are bones but clappers to the bells of brawn?
Who are stones and rainbows but gall and glory?
The man who leaps from an upper storey
and falls at our feet is my done-for dread.

So hammer, hooves; the holes you hatch
will jump with embryos whose tears
of joy will spurt a second flood
for hands and ankles that throb like hearts.

Stink, fine customhouse, the rags of duty
stop your toilet, no bird with tonsilitis;
but pebbles smuggled, the shining rocks
of the crushed moon, kindle our parlors.

Enraged swans bathing in beauty's scar
left in the distance by an amputated geyser
change the argument of our geography:
ah everything swims in the lake of an eye!

The haze on the hill is there to take you from me,
I pluck you back on the sting of a stem,
while here every object turns into its opposite,
and there every sound contains your haw and hem.

Oh we bump to your hovel, two tough customers,
cocky as gobs with bullet-proof bibs,
but act like gawks when caught with the goods
as you spring a first line, sweet crossexamination.

So gear us a game, or a freight-train story
of sociologic lies, the brain you stumped a toe on,
or grammar they hung up your ace-in-the-hole coat on,
or love with closed eyes that your hot hand spewed!

Girl At The Window

On her heart's little harp
she plunked a tune for the amethyst crows,
birds that fell like pieces of night
to fleck the diadem of day.

But the crows flew away.
What a deafening noise! they said.

And I thought I sighed such a soft note, said she.
But to the birds it must have been loud,
loud as the wind of the past is to me.

Song Without A Singer

To carefully fold the old insides,
and set the trunk on a hill of water,
and watch the day die as if it were Someone,
and sleep by yourself as though you weren't there.

To be lost as a tune hummed once,
and never found, like a lone ruby berry,
hunted by the babyless, listless lady,
combing her hair of wind.

To stumble on the past, without recognizing it,
and dream of the future as though it were gone . . .
Home! cried the hawk, and I said, Where?
and the butterfly sauntered by a rusty old gun.

Matin Pour Matta

When the foot opens like a cup
miles and miles go in a gulp.

When the hand's teeth drop out,
what no hand can chew begins to sprout.

But no optical rake or hoe
prepares the ground for what you do not know.

The breathless rock that swims
eludes all synonyms.

If the lips of the chest move with milk
cats from other countries learn to talk.

When knives are exhaled like words,
wounds flow with thoughts of birds.

And the breath you failed to catch
will hide in your hair like a bat.

This is what I write
on a page torn from the scalp of night:

When you split the world in two,
one half lives, the other dies for you.

Poem For Paul Eluard

The clouds of dissipation hang like wars
in the peaceful sky of my heart's-ease;
the warning birds of wisdom let fall the stars
of their cries in the midst of escaping streets.

The winds of will confabulate,
the clouds grow blacker as if choking;
children gesticulate like toys
as the guns of weather joking.

When my nerves' rain inhabits me,
the salt birds of the brain will melt,
the wind will trickle to the ground,
and underneath the violent tree

the dead cat will be found,
whose eyes looked out from every pore,
and buried (oh, the bone of lust!)
by children who never mourned before.

Poem For Aglaya

Heaven crawls with the world's great ghost,
ants of the alphabet travel like pollen,
punctual as fear, drag at the body of noon
and hide that nameless face in midnight's ditch.

What is larger than memory?
Memory is the ocean that drinks its own tears.

If the tree faints in my arms,
if my ears drop off like nuts,
will you make a nest with your hands?
Then I'll lay my two eyes at your feet
as a duck lays eggs in sweet grass.

Sweet grass that grows in me,
let my sweetheart trust your pillow,
for she's the antidote to the poisoned pool,
home of immune fish, my bedfellows.

POEMS FOR PAINTERS

Flag Of Ecstasy

for Marcel Duchamp

Over the towers of autoerotic honey
Over the dungeons of homicidal drives

Over the pleasures of invading sleep
Over the sorrows of invading a woman

Over the voix céleste
Over vomito negro

Over the unendurable sensation of madness
Over the insatiable sense of sin

Over the spirit of uprisings
Over the bodies of tragediennes

Over tarantism: "melancholy stupor and an uncontroll-
    able desire to dance"
Over all

Over ambivalent virginity
Over unfathomable succubi

Over the tormentors of Negresses
Over openhearted sans-culottes

Over a stactometer for the tears of France
Over unmanageable hermaphrodites

Over the rattlesnake sexlessness of art lovers
Over the shithouse enigmas of art-haters

Over the sun's lascivious serum
Over the sewage of the moon

Over the saints of debauchery
Over criminals made of gold

Over the princes of delirium
Over the paupers of peace

Over signs foretelling the end of the world
Over signs foretelling the beginning of a world

Like one of those tender strips of flesh
On either side of the vertebral column

Marcel, wave!

Serenade To Leonor

Lion-girl of the Rue Payenne
Is that your mate with the mauve mouth who wants in?

Face powder settles on the brows of the walls
While hair from the tap flows into fingerbowls

Your first breast is the envy of all paradoxes
Invisible dainty spiders eat holes in your stockings

As you step from one room's hemisphere to another
Your second breast wrangles with a young bat's brother

It's all you can do to prove you're not his sister
Before he goes you'll give him a devious picture

If he looks through the evening's window upside down
Glue a smile on his back, on his knee a frown

When he gazes at the moon's mirror wrongside up
Will you make his tongue spin like a star or a top?

Oh your tricks are as real as a clock striking four
Your perfume bottles fill with the breath of this paramour

Your talons dyed with blue, the blue tears of night
Scratch at his eyes with unexpected daylight

As the cat with the violet lips leaps in
To visit the lion-girl of the Rue Payenne

O

for Estéban

O seditious toxins of nostalgia
Found at the foot of the first fruits of love!

Mamelukes of primeval palmistry
Abandon the cross of highhanded talismen
Giants of inertia are fed through the nose
Insatiable as a woman on the eve of execution
Chang and Eng revive, injured with enjoyment

And the whole world is like a larva laid in space
Nowhere to be seen is the obsolete practice of
   self-cremation
Debased spectacular energy is turned into poetry

The Septembrists of a new carnality
Hold hands with numerological images
Eruptive as religion, evocative as touch

Stupors of the most omnivorous colors
Envelop beholders of crime in the name of country
Now comes the promise of an indefinable sickness
Sweet as the vision of a child plotting murder
Epochs of agony dissolve like charley horses

O sulphuric carols of revulsion and invention
Found at the foot of nowhere-to-go!

Great are the castoff secrets of suffering
Raw the interchangeable parts of pleasure
A pile of stars, providential as ova
Necropolis of vulpine nights — o undermining
Dream! . . . Monstrous mother of subliminal scavengers
Even Fear has not such strong-arm pariahs
Undisguised as the virus of nothingness
Rialtos revel in reptilian transfusions

There's No Place To Sleep In This Bed, Tanguy

The storks like elbows had a fit of falling
She beat me over the head with a lung
Somewhere a voice is calling Picasso
And the lasso of love has the ghost of a chance

The bewildering pathos of a bag of china candy
The hole in the rock where the sea lost hope
The faceless spectators whose tears have no shadows
Ah for this and these my poems are undone

There's no place to sleep in this bed, Tanguy
The wires are cut that connect us with slumber
And the number of day and the number of night is one!
Those grains of sand are menacing as statues

Fountains of fire await the painted trigger
And the nails you drove in the earth have sprung up
Madonnas and torture-machines tell the time
You touch a cloud the rain becomes an object

Whose bow is the rainbow whose arrow is Egypt
Whose target unknown whose quarry is fear
For these are skeletons we never saw before
With skins like candies and no tongue to toss on

You've set new traps for ancient dreams
Oh tame them and train them before they get caught!
There's no place to sleep in this bed, Tanguy
There are too many monuments of broken hearts

SLEEP IN A NEST OF FLAMES

I Wonder

Where do we go from here?
The wind is small enough to hide beneath a stone,
The eye sharp enough cuts the world to the core,
The bird of darkness pecks out the moon
And one of the five fingers finds a fifth season.

So where do we go from here?
I walk in dew, you walk in blood,
I pick a flower, you lift a hand
And the hand leaves the body as the flower leaves the land,
And the dew is blood and the blood is dew.

Now where do we go from here?
Yes, the wind is small! The world is stone
And harder than stone not to break in two;
The body face down plants a tongue in the ground,
A tongue as red as the morning dew!

But where do we go from here?
The eye, most marvelous of marvelous mirrors,
Falls in the net of that other acrobat,
The spider, the spider twines it about;
The spider watches the sun go down.

And where do we go from here?
The eagle asleep in the nest of roses
Is not an eagle, is not a nest!
While bees draw blood for the honeycomb,
Dead hands sweat again, like plants.

Then where do we go from here?
The cry in the forest knocks an ear from the tree,
The bird chips a cheek from the headless flower;
The neckless fish turns its head like a bird,
And the worm sings louder than ever before:

Tell me, where do we go from here?
The herd that lives on time and space

(With horns of the dead, hooves of the quick)
Returns like yesterday, now and tomorrow
To lick the salt of the salt heart's face!

But where are you going? I asked the thief.
To steal the real from unreality:
I'll carve the apple from the flesh of its lip,
Count the gold kisses and stop the blood
With another kiss like a wound on a wound!

And where are you bound? I asked the assassin.
To kill the bride of my best friend, Night.
Fear is her name. And then?
And then? Ah, then my desire will flow
With flaming tears to make her body glow!

And where are you going? I stopped a beggar.
To write a poem, the beggar said.
It's all I've left of pride, he said,
And what will the bird of the poem sing?
About a beggar who killed a king!

And why do you hurry? I asked a rich man.
To spend as little as I can
For as much as I can get:
The little love that I will save
Should be enough to dig my grave.

Why does the world run, mother, mother?
The world runs to keep from falling
But the wind is looking for nothing at all —
The clouds are looking for the wind
And your own heart set the world a-spinning.

Will father come home? The gnome often wondered:
And followed his tracks — but he walked backwards;
And listened for his voice — he held his breath;

Then nailed a letter to a tree by the way,
But the tree's tears washed the words away.

Is that you, brother? Where are you headed?
There's a head in my heart that drinks my blood!
On my head there's a heart like a wounded hat!
The head in my hands (oh, it fell at my feet)
I'll throw to the first beheaded man I meet!

Sister, child, where do you go?
To wrap myself in the warm fur of night —
It's snowing, you see. Oh
Look how the statues catch the falling petals!
Hear! how the skinless beast of the day is howling!

Come live with me . . . I begged Someone.
Come live with me! Someone replied.
Her face was turned away from me
But I knew by the bracelet of bones at her side
That the voice of her breast was the echo of my own.

Oh where shall we go? I turned to the sky.
The sky, as if frightened by my sudden words,
Started to pull all the clouds away.
"You might as well stay!" — Was it Someone? — No one!
The hand had fallen, a bracelet of words.

What time is it? What's the time?
The earth turned over on its other side.
The wind came out from underneath a stone.
The cat awoke in its nest of roses
And soared like an eagle with a wreath of red bones.

Where are you and where am I?
This is the season the fifth finger found.
Are these tears fruit of a tree growing there?
No! these are tears that water the tongue
Planted in the ground by a head face down.

71

Was the tongue as red as the morning dew?
The morning dew was red, red,
And the tongue was red as flame,
And the tree that grows will be red as a rose,
A rose as red as the world aflame!

Ballad For Baudelaire

"Baudelaire blanc, Baudelaire noir,
jour et nuit le même diamant, dégagé
des poussières de la mort."

PAUL ELUARD

For this man shed no tear,
For him the whole world is a tear!
The world to his clairvoyant eye,
A crystal swarming with eternity!
All the children, animals that we were,
Stretch out their arms as to a guiding star!
The murderer and the accursed
Undo the murder and invert the curse!
The Treasury and the full jail's doors
Burst, their inmates' innocence restored!
All the beggars and all the thieves
Try again their pride and their release!
The violent martyr and the meek avenger
Relive the hours of their splendor!
The drunkard in his trembling trance
Strikes light from the stone of chance!
The old old women and the old men
Catch fire from each other's eyes again!
Lovers in their beds of grief and delight
Know the secret of death and the secret of life!
Even the skeleton with nonchalant purity
Usurps the elegance of any posing beauty!
The sickly pilgrim at the dried up spring
Startles more milk than he can drink!
The fullest heart is the first to pour.
Les charmes de l'horreur n'enivrent que les forts!
Prophets trailing their robes of agony
Rejoice in famine and weep in plenty!
Whores in body and whores in soul
Exchange places and curse the day's deal!
Madmen, exiles of the mind,
Assimilate their newfound land!
Death itself like a long-held place

73

Is stormed and taken, glorified at last!
Poets, enemies of peace,
Dream of armies swallowed by the sea!
A girl on the road to the town of Pity
Meets and marries a man from Cruel City!
Memory, ghost of everyone, does no harm,
Sits quietly at the table, eating his own heart!
The moonlit grave of the alchemist opens,
His closed bone hands are golden roses!
Pleasure, rollicking beast, has eaten
The bitter nut that makes his tooth sweeter!
Pain in a white dress mourns the more,
Despair in summer has harvested the snow!
A fountain of blood, rumored in the wood,
Stains the doorsteps with brotherhood!
The cripple's crutch, the blindman's stick,
Feed the last flame of the last clinic!
Disease, like a fabulous butterfly,
Is mounted on a pin for all to admire!
The house of commons and the house of lords
Hang themselves from their ropes of words!
Men are caught in nets until
Mermaids, never caught, are seen at will!
The phantom rebel with a key of flesh and bone
Melts the lock of the millennium!
The son, a prisoner of paradise,
Finds his freedom in patricide!
Winding in and out of these
The wind of the wilderness scatters its seeds!
Standing in the street, a single-minded man
Multiplies himself until he's back where he began!
A wingless horse heard the story one day
Of a horse with wings and flew away!
Clouds compounding the past and future
Dissolve in tears as if they never were!
A dog romping in the field of battle
Never knew hide-and-seek to be so terrible!
The hunchback watching the children pass

Hurls his hump as if his house were glass!
How is the last mother like the first?
How many new worlds to the universe!
Freaks of fancy and the housewife's norm
Meet in a dungeon to plot against the home!
Ocean and desert, long-lost brothers,
The day will dawn when you will greet each other!
The moon, half white, half black,
Looks in vain for white folk and black!
Dust of the sun and no one to sweep.
But glory comes later — first the dream!
The map on a bird's breast will do, will do
To guide you far from the tried and true!
Though every nation fall and the leaves,
New years rise like a single tree!
Life is an old man, Love is a woman,
Their child is Death, for their child is human!
Neither soul nor body of longing or disgust
Knows when the last kiss changes to the first!
The wine of horror intoxicates the strong,
A drop of water could move the world around!
Laugh if you can, weep if you must
At all that once was nothing, at everything that's dust!
But for this man, shed no tear,
For him the whole world is a tear!
Soît-il noir, soît-il blanc
Jour et nuit le même diamant!
The world to his clairvoyant eye
A crystal swarming with eternity!

Xmas Gift

*"Come to our conveniently located store ...
and pick out in a few minutes a nice
assortment of jokes, tricks, puzzles,
pocket games and novelties. Our vast
assortment of different items are sure
to please your soldier."*

ADVT.

"Pet her, pink him, play pranks with them."

FINNEGANS WAKE

THE PROLOGUE

O you clown! with your stick candy vices
You let us sin without our knowing it
The pop of your paddle or paperbag
Shocks us into the nonsense trance

How nearly alike are the evil and funny
And how we love and laugh at them both
And cry too! No one knows
When the clown's capers will move us to tears

What whore is not mocked at? Even when painted
Up like a clown she's loved like a loved one
What can make us smile any quicker
Than ugliness? Not beauty — beauty breaks the heart

Ugliness puts it together again
That old woman fallen in the gutter
Is she laughing or crying?
Does she make us weep or gruesomely grin?

The sinister is saved by a sense of humor
But love is lost. Who could love Ophelia
After she went mad? It was not her death
That was tragic, death was her due

It's the property of the old too
But stolen goods for the young and whole
Poverty is laugh-provoking. Why?
Clowns in rags are most effective
Clowns in riches are affected

THE PACKAGE

(1) *joke*
Along came a member of the human race
He had no heart and he had no face
He had no soul and he had no body
This can't be me, he said, by golly!

(2) *trick*
If I can't have it all, half of it will do
If I can't have half then give me a quarter
The more it disappears, the greater the craving
In a minute there'll be nothing left but the gravy

(3) *puzzle*
Captain and his men ride along in a tank
Captain sticks his head out, off it came
Captain falls back in the arms of a Looey
Doctor try to find out why that Looey's looney

(4) *pocket game*
Clench your hand in an empty pocket
The neck of nothing will gasp for air
If you squeeze it hard and long enough
There'll even be blood — surely something was
    there

(5) *novelty*
Here's a paper doll that you can call your own
Instead of a dollar mark there's a skull and cross-
    bones

77

Though she looks lugubrious there's life in the
  old girl yet
Just strike a match to her and watch her choke
  to death

(6) *joke*

Now here's some things I knew before
A forest fire must start with a tree
You risk your life — but not for me
We pay to live — but we can die free

(7) *trick*

Fire upon the clocks of war!
When bullets fix the time of day
It's very apt to stay that way
(Until the generals wind some more)

(8) *puzzle*

How did this skeleton get in here?
"Hold it to the mirror" — Christ, it looks like
  me!
"Now take a look at yourself in there"
Damned if we don't make a pair

(9) *pocket game*

Eye in the labyrinth! Roll it around
Until you see things upside down
All the gold will be blood then
And the dead come marching down the
  mountains

(10) *novelty*

King Midas was a happy man indeed
With his golden roses and gold daughter
The things we lay our eyes on crumble
Things we touch begin to bleed

(11) *joke*

Love is a little girl walking down the street
She comes back this way and doesn't seem so
    sweet
I hate to see her walking down that street once
    more
The next time she walks by she'll be a full-fledged
    whore

(12) *trick*

Suppose we change places, the enemy and I
That's an ancient trick though it's never worked
As long as we have to fight we'll find we want to
Whether I think you're me or you think I'm you

(13) *puzzle*

All the gloom of winter is held in the sun's hand
All of war's horror is in the heart of peace
"The battle's over!" the winner shouts
The vanquished vows it's just begun

(14) *pocket game*

A pretty glass! On one side a good face
The other looks rather like the devil . . .
Hold it to the light, look at both sides a while:
What a sad clown it makes — the devil's lost his
    smile

(15) *novelty*

Heaven's not made of fire and pain
(Neither was home, neither was home)
In Heaven blood doesn't rain for rain
The way it does here . . . So this is Hell!

CARD OF THANKS

Thanks for the package, dear sir or madam
You knew what you were sending
I'm keeping all these little things
When the war's all over I'll pack them away
I might have a son myself some day

Jokes, tricks, puzzles, pocket games and novelties
Are just what it takes to please your soldier
There's nothing we want more than clowns and whores
(Except perhaps to know what it is we're fighting for)

So thank you very much, dear sir or madam
The bells of hell ring ting-a-ling for me
Whether I die or whether they miss me
O clowns in rags, you're most affected
Clowns in riches are protected

Thank you again, and sleep well

Epigrams

Dripping with sleep I went to write a poem
And the waters of the world took me for their own.

I

I love my animal heart
Although he fool me and hide
The happier I to find him alive
Though he leap at another and pretend I'm a stranger.

II

Happy? The eye of the world
Is so red with blood the sun itself
Will never be pure again
Purity? Pshaw! Prurient.

III

The feet of his days have been mangled
And the knees gone blind
The greater the love the deeper the desolation
And night's bright tongue licks everything.

IV

Pleasure boat, pleasure boat where has it gone?
To the bottom of the black river, like a white bone
What drowned dog will break a tooth upon it?
Who in the dying crowd stops a love sonnet?

V

Tender blows the leaf, tender drops the eye
And the wind wounds and the rain heals

And death goes on forever
And life almost like it was before.

VI

Do birds need to fly so much
Or do they just want to?
Do soldiers need to die so much
Or were they just told to?

VII

Andromache, I think of you!
When war goes on forever
And life almost as it was before
Tell me tales that dead men tell, there are no more.

VIII

Let us make of day a delirium
And of the night a theatre of desire
The more emotions we know
The more scientific we can be about them.

IX

Simple is madness, like a kick in the pants
That's what you think
The city crumbles under the very eyes
Of Time. History stinks!

X

So you'd eat the ear of Van Gogh!
Suicides and paupers cram your cellars:
Let this poem be your bedfellow
And the reins of nightmare break.

XI

Little lamb who made thee?
Ho but the egg is growing hair
Look, the flowers show their teeth and tongues
Little lamb, you seem so right, miracles so
   wrong.

ABC's

for the child of no one, who grows up to look like everyone's son

A

Ask horror for a helping hand,
peel the glove to fit your own:
feel his heart of shifting sands
turn to a lake of stone.

a

B

Bring to her senses the insulting rose
who moves like the muscles of your mouth;
reveal how a hardier flower grows,
loving a fool to death.

b

C

Careen the animal that roams like sound,
bodiless as the voice of rot,
from the lithe swallow that won't go down
to the tear that won't come up.

c

D

Drive the demon who preys on sleep
up the avenue of fame;
marry the match to the dustheap
and a child will jump from the flame.

d

E

Excuse the hereditary hump,
inmate of the pleasant breast;
every lunge of the brain's bright lamp
rocks a young maniac to rest.

e

F

Find for the finger the ring that broke
and stiffened to a nail;
find for the tree the missing stroke,
and the cloud lost in the mail.

f

G

Guarantee to birds at odds
beautiful eyes to peck;
days that drift from dawn to dark
hang about their necks.

g

H

Headfirst is the way we're born,
graved feet forward, lucky dead;
but oh the motions we'll have known
when all is done and said!

h

I

Inflamed with solitude, a girl
may break a dish as though it were a law;
hold to the landscape color of a curl,
and out will come the face you thought you saw.

i

J

Jagged as the moon, a boy's desire
may break a dish as though it were a toy;
thrilled to see the insect suddenly expire
he hunts himself, a fugitive from joy.

j

K

Kinky as blood, the gutter feeds
on words that look like waste;

garbage on which the mind may bleed
dwells flagrantly chaste.

k

L

Lift the illogical contraband
from your favorite brute;
footlights follow those who can,
blackouts swallow those who won't.

l

M

M is for the muse of murder:
money: melancholy: mirth:
masks for gas police the power
that anagrams your date of birth.

m

N

Nothing, nothing is so valuable
as freedom, Dante said.
Nothing, nothing is less haveable:
ask anyone. Dante's dead.

n

O

Oh, for some other fear than this!
Love is leaving town.
But think of the things you might have missed
if death hadn't shown you around.

o

P

Pain is the proper helpmeet
to get a lusty poem by;
but there's no telling if he
won't live to hit you in the eye.

p

Q

Quatrains such as these are quick
but quicker far the tension
that takes possession of my stalk
when the turtle-bud is shaken.

q

R

Rest awhile! You rush like sun
over the insurmountable future.
Will me a memory to run
the other way — to meet you.

r

S

Struck with the bargains bodies drive,
empty the image from your head;
when the twin is magnetized,
both will infect the bed.

s

T

Trapeze of the unconscious whim
attracts the derelict acrobat
whose abstractions prove to him
imagination's This and That.

t

U

Undo the hortatory worm
from the carcass of despair.
Though unsupported as the earth,
thought is horned as the hare.

u

V

Vary the quarantine of night,
loose a plague on the healthy day:

sun only makes the moon more white
and drives the stars away.

v

W

Worn-out afternoons are good
to stuff an imaginary snake.
Forgotten men of the prisoned blood
cohort the heart's jailbreak.

w

X

X is the quantity found by finding
the doubles of good and bad:
handsprings handcuffed, or turning
a fancy-free flip and a half.

x

Y

Y is the year you are treading:
time's teeth level with your lips!
Horror's helping heart already
congeals our fingertips.

y

Z

Zero hours zinc the throat
of time the drunkard every day;
oh how to sober him up before
he dreams the dream away?

z

THE BREATHLESS ROCK THAT SWIMS

I Was In Paris Again Last Night

I was in Paris again last night
Deep in the marvelous manmade wood
Where the roads lead back to the roads
And you want to be lost forever.

This Is The Rock

This is the rock
to lie upon,
waiting to pluck
fire from sun.

Press arms down,
lay your head upon it:
not again will sun
be so hot and quiet.

Somewhat Monday

there is a hill here and the green blades slyly with nostalgia
a mockingbird says *aw now aw now* with eyes congealing drops
    of sweat

i find no fault with the snakes lovely
or why reproach a petal for its perfectness
there are worse things than a hawk's swiftness
there is an icy image latent and the phlegm of drudgery in
    throats and throats

Optional

foreword

persimmons are on the trees on the quaggy ground too do not eat
one that isn't soft for it will pucker your mouth but anyway you
are beautiful whether your mouth is puckered or not

POEM

o maleness of lovers or animals kisses oh bitter (as orangepeel) and
    seekers of forests o brass and footprints

i run with slow steps and am aroused from a narcosis of squalor

my hands are warmed on icy foreheads and my thighs made cold
    with consecrate lusts
ochrefaced men move into a numbness
why am i hostile to the keepers of gardens and the keepers of
    cities
an existence is nullified in the omega of a cracked hickorynut

let only a tree be your lover
take only sand for a marriagebed
use sun for raiment and rain for a sacrament
rain rages on the riversurface

rain pursues a vagrancy and is an impetus for death by drowning

Left Instantly Designs

describe the circles
first; terror
will stay and
the moon displace

them and control
the rain;
then walk away
in the rain's disgrace;

the blood's obedience
will follow
instantly designs
left in the sky's hollow;

once fearful often
each ear then
accepts its
rightful coffin;

if the dream
cries, let
the moon mother
it, encircled

with goodbyes
mist
cannot
smother;

explain your circles
to the sun
and, but for the dark,
run.

I Open My Eye

Roses blew up like paper bags,
knives and forks are melted down,
the four-o'clocks were soundproof
and the cut hair scattered.
Grandmother, like a sewing machine, struck four,
and that was the end of her.

Songs grew ripe on the chinaberry tree,
daddy grew rigid as a nickel,
mother was a rose, not thorny as a bee though,
the fire in the fireplace was a clown without a clown's
    face.

Why Ears

why should you lie dead
at ten o'clock then carelessly
talk and rise into a gold awakening

then (tell me) why
should you as fondling
a sprig of heliotrope
draw in the scent through
two
chiseled
nostrils

why are you never specific

the morning is definite the wind is
you
are a ghost on horseback
or the image of a hotness caught in ice
you are the loophole in a hangrope
and i forever harmonious
discords sagging about your head and ears

I Wouldn't Put It Past You

And you may not have hair as curly as the alphabet
but if your googoo eyes were a bundle of germs
there'd be an epidemic.
With your greenhorn complexion
and your grasswidow ways
you'd make a butcher kill a granite cow
and weigh the gravel out for hamburger.
I mean you'd start the eskimos stripteasing,
give dummies the shakes,
get flyingcircuses to crawl on their hands and knees.
No I wouldn't put it past you.
Just let somebody set you on the fence,
by gosh foulballs would be annulled
and home-runs the rule.
The weather forecast that overlooked you, baby,
sure better watch out for the next cyclone,
seeing how my uptown's flattened,
and my downtown a-waving in the wind.

It Seems You Never Were

Should every object claim a place to fit
Simply because your absence caused it?

Strange how all of you fits in the cup
I lift to my lips. As I drink you down
It seems you never were, but the way I walk
Tells me I'm drunk with the thought of you alone.
Your heart in my breast as if it were my own
Crooks its foot to cage the tiger's tears.
It seems you never were! And when I drown today
Though I find you fishing on every shore
No heart but my heart will make you live once more.

To Be Pickled In Alcohol

I

if brains pickled in alcohol prove anything don't say sweetly *it
    may be hurtin you but it's killin me*
words said sweetly said even nicely are not an antitoxin

here is a tic for your nose and cheek and a paperhat to be gay with
o fingers and the twitching of a head
you will know the glued standing and see many locomotives
    rush to a destruction

II

i rumble on the narrow streets and find an expiation for this chaos
he said *it's red like that all over looking* and i choked a cigarette
    butt
looking in my glass i am sure that i resemble a traffic squall or a
    sudden snow
a promise has been too insistent and i mold stickily bread into a
    hanging
if a watch ticks shatter your unrest against abnormality

who has said a gray day now is a penitent

i hold tightly to an ivy wreath and a shudder
with torn nails i build grandly the last madhouse for a burned
    dream

Your Horoscope

CAPRICORNUS

Manifest exemplary cussedness if you wish to get through this quarter with a minimum of Fortune's blows.

The loophole of self-pollution could save you from a tyrannical sweetness.

You may witness the annual deflowering of the daughter of the King of Demons. "My name's Dreamily," she'll say when it's half over.

Prepare yourself for a season that's misshapen, like the stones from which we sprang.

AQUARIUS

If spiritual doldrums are encountered, avoid camp followers, palmists and bicycle instructors.

Lucky number: the last two figures on your electric light bill.

Omit having shoes shined by bootblacks with a knowledge of lingua franca.

The next time you behold the unnatural, no use to exult; your fellow-creature disenchantment isn't gone yet.

PISCES

Those wishing to bring discredit upon their families should fix themselves elflocks — every other midnight.

Yearning for dismemberment will do you no harm.

Impartial vituperation may solve things.

Combat what may easily become your besetting sin: bestiality with a dildo.

ARIES

If your feigning of beatitude is prolonged, you risk disfigurement.

The exorcist will be taken in, provided an unbecoming modesty is assumed.

It may or may not be beneficial to solve conundrums invented by cranky seamstresses.

Though a second offender, you will go free to offend again.

TAURUS

Unless exalted by degradation, uplift will get you nowhere.

Experiment with rudimentary wonder-working on Tuesdays.

A gentleman with a diploma in Egyptology (or some related source) may turn out to be a swine.

Ignore court summonses, unless written acrostically.

GEMINI

Benevolent auditory omen: stellar zooms.

You'll find yourself most susceptible to corrective agents if mood is neither vitriolic nor easygoing, but betwixt and between.

While awaiting a state of dejection, do without rollcalls, palliatives, and candidates for office.

Minus misgivings, switch your favorite hurtful pastime from self-denial to exchanging clouts with former schoolmates.

CANCER

First quarter earmarked for explosive situations: be catlike.

Recommended motto for those suffering from self-improvement: "O flesh, farewell!"

Third quarter, permit yourself to be as deceitful as a coiffeur with cold curling irons.

Shun coal-oil lamps, dragnets, and anchorites with athlete's foot.

LEO

Fathomless period of indolence. Only if you aspire to a knight-errant evil-doing will you hit bottom; otherwise expect to remain as moody as a drudge.

Thursdays propitious for body snatching.

Time to correct two minor vices: detestable cheeriness and love of disciplinary measures.

If you dream of a grizzly bear clasping lemon blossoms, your mental make-up is changing for the better.

VIRGO

During chance commitment to penitentiary, comfort yourself with being the most impenitent.

Beware of those criminologists and contortionists whose fluids are excited by impromptu autopsies.

If there's a new moon (and you believe it's new), erlking strivings should be discouraged.

When you hear the last words of the last druid spoken in dream, don't answer back.

LIBRA

In case you find yourself wanting either to marry, or to be, a lumberjack, you'll find yourself wanting.

Artifice holds realistic potentialities.

Wear that badge of waywardness. Nothing will happen.

If you want to get rich, you'll stop wanting, when you do.

SCORPIO

Though insensitive to all deterrents, you'll wind up the first quarter charmed as a well-fed derelict.

A reign of torpor will begin.

Verdict: for acquittal. The charge: none.

The reign of torpor may end as imperceptibly as the death of a missing person whom you believed to be dead already.

SAGITTARIUS

Don't be surprised to discover yourself capable of dog-like affection when bedevilled.

Prevailing mood: expectation of uprisings.

It will do no good to change your status from that of Non-combattant in the war against the Social Evil to that of Volunteer in the semi-barbaric squadron of Posthypnotic Safeblowers.

Your happiness: illusory as a killer in repose.

DRAWINGS

This Is A Prosaic Age

Our tribal chants are advertising slogans. A runic melody is almost unheard of.

I do not remember when the last auction of beasts for new heralds was held. The *démon particulier* is almost extinct.

At the wishing well, boys and girls wish for each other, that's all. This is a prosaic age.

Who would think of composing a vade mecum for a star the shape of you? We have precepts for good driving, but no one gets a citation for a few simple words grouped in an evocative way.

If the poetry of the earth is more precious than gold, how poor we are! If the poetry of heaven is more powerful than man-made explosives, we are weak, Lord.

I built for you a song to be looked at in your sleep. "Architect unknown" you noted in your diary next morning. Would you like to know how it feels to have a nail driven in your shadow by mistake? It feels the same as though the nail were planted there on purpose. That is the way things are in this prosaic age.

How Two Words Coming Together May Make Poetry Aside From Their Practical Meaning: Sign Painted Large On Front of Truck:

B E L L
m o v i n g

Poem From The Insurance Policy Of The Automobile Club Of New York, Inc.

For Loss of

    Life
    Two Eyes
    Two Arms
    Two Hands
    Two Legs
    Two Feet
    One Arm and One Leg
    One Arm and One Foot
    One Hand and One Foot
    One Leg and One Eye
    One Arm and One Eye
    One Hand and One Eye
    One Foot and One Eye
    One Arm
    One Hand
    One Leg
    One Foot
    One Eye

Hotel Poem

I decided to make a list of a hundred hotels, and here is the way
it began:

> Hotel of the Numbered Days
> Hotel of Strange Bodies and Narrow Escapes
> Hotel Every Man for Himself
> Hotel of the Hobbled Heart
> Hotel of Weather Disturbances
> Hotel of the Prize Pony
> Hotel of Crime Against Children
> Dismantled Cathedral Hotel
> Hotel Humbug
> Hotel of the High Spots
> Hotel of Young Poets
> Nothing Doing Hotel
> Hotel One-Thirty P.M.
> Hotel Lingo
> Hotel Havoc
> Hydraulic Hotel
> Self-Portrait Hotel
> Hotel of the Hurting Eyes
> Modern Love Hotel
> The Terrible Hotel
> Taken By Surprise Hotel
> Hotel of Generous Proportions
> Hotel of the Tough Baby
> Hotel Breast of Veal
> Hotel Jumping-off Place
> Hotel Sinister Character
> Hotel Bride-to-Be, Hotel of Sudden Death

that's as far as I got.

Flowers Without Eyes

The most sensitive flowers are blind. I do not say this is true of people. It is certainly not true of flies.

When I looked at the shape of the cut-out space down the middle of my razorblade, I visualized a bannister shaped that way. When I looked 'bannister' up in the dictionary (to see how to spell it) I found that the original word is *baluster*. When I looked up 'baluster' I found that the word has travelled from the Greek *balaustion* to the Latin *balaustium* (and on through the Italian and French). *Balaustium* means: wild pomegranate flower.

I am almost sure that wild pomegranate flowers cannot see.

Souvenir De Jouvet

What is this You?

We are mudpies of Time but that is not all. We are clocks of flesh and blood but that is not all. I remember how you disappeared but I do not know how you may reappear.

When I die, who will say, That is not he? I say, This body may be yours but it is not You. I ask, Where are you gone? Is the sun gone when it goes behind a cloud?

And this mask we knew as Louis Jouvet? Magnificent disguise! But not created for the cosmic tour.

Message For Rimbaud

Your summerhouse of underdone meat is still standing, boy. The last time I went by, a note was tacked on the door. It read, "Bleed for me!" There was no signature, but I recognized Humanity's handwriting.

Chanson Pour Billie

Whoa, hillbilly, you've got me where you want me — in the ferris wheel of that fraudulent wail. Like a baptized woman in a moment of depravity, your voice rings out, headstrong and dreamy.

On a night of desperadoes, you deliver the clearcut message from the anti-suicides. In the cobalt of morning, your half-breed brothers find you and put you to bed tenderly, as though you were their little dead sister.

The distress we feel in your presence is like hearing footsteps that will take us away, or reading a threat in an unknown handwriting, or seeing a guttersnipe die for a fetish.

To me, gringo of your insolence, you are the hardhearted gypsy, disreputable as pleasure, to whom I cast myself off like a drug from the brain. Your grenadine gums are exciting as a holdup. It would not matter if your songs were in Cantonese.

Popular as crime, you've created an army, derelicts who await the freight of a midnight egocentric singing. It would not matter if your songs were a flying machine.

Hipped as a gangster you go your heartrending way, and give us gooseflesh because we cannot possess you. Though we throw ourselves at your feet you grunt like a mother or a chunky Cherokee in front of something uneatable.

In an atmosphere of drowning, your eggplant lyrics save our hungry lives. On a grown-up dismal day your Bedouin children bring contraband sunshine.

In the factory of contagions that douse the world with dusky honeydew, and dupe the studious into getaways, and jerk to his feet the horsewhipped hooligan, how about giving us a job to do? Something secretive and unhygienic — housebreaker, cardsharper, anything you say — so long as the boss can be Billie Holiday.

The Impossility Of Dying In Your Arms
Does Not Sadden Me

I do not want to be told any more of your facts! I cannot abide any more of your fantasy! I'm in the doldrums, birthplace of hurricanes.

How senseless, the sermons of stones . . . But the poet's poem may be disinterested as the action of an enzyme. "It is sweet," said Laotse, tasting the vinegar.

Reptilia

The way a tongue darts from a crack in chaos. The way nothing
is ever the same. The way you do what you find yourself doing.
The way nothing matters. The way sleep rusts the soul. The way
nothing is ever understood. The way sleep sharpens time. The
way nothing happens. The way she poisons a cup of coffee. The
way nothing can help. The way he walks. The way nothing was
said. The way babies are born. The way nothing changes. The
way it starts to rain. The way nothing could be done. The way to
make love. The way nothing stays still. The way roads go wind-
ing. The way nothing remains.

THE END OF THE WORLD
IS BEAUTIFUL TODAY

Sonnet

(for Pavlik's exhibition, Rome 1950)

What kind of poem would I like to write?
One in which the images are new
and yet fill one with pleasure, like a face
that's strange but which we recognize with joy
mixed with nostalgia. When the thick blood
of winter's cut like a cake by the sun's gold knife —
have a piece! It's the birthday of the world.
A lamb may sing like a bird, a bird may bleat;
flowers smile as though no one were poor;
oxen make an inarticulate
music as if no one were too rich.
One ear is not less awesome than a pair.
What kind of poem would you like to read?
What kind of life is there still left to lead?

The Dead Spring

By whose order does the drizzling eye,
A winter wound shrinking in the glare of spring,
Fix the game blood galloping, galloping
From head to foot of the sad spraddling farm?

Let the smoke flurry though it leave the lungs
Crisp as cinders, charred as twin stars
Lured from their orbit by the voice of the void.
Let the clouds play as if nothing were decaying!

I sing the dead spring fooling us all with flowers.
I praise the gruesome hour,
Fascinated by the dangle of its own bones' music,
And the wind, that infinite corpse
Whose ghost is now perfume, now rot.

I am sure I heard the rat of death last night
Drilling the last door of the heart's desire.
I am sure that he will get what he was grinding for.
Spring is not my cat.

The Half-Thoughts, The Distances Of Pain

To Edith Sitwell

The half-thoughts, the distances of pain!
Have you heard the bird that groans at the sight of death
Have you seen the insect cursing its color
Have you known a cloud to balk at the smallest breath
Has grass never struggled to die while green

The half-thoughts, the distances of pain!
The bat tormented in the hair of day
Deceitful night, emptying her heart of sleep
And they say the cricket was a butterfly
Who traded her wings for speech

The half-thoughts, the distances of pain!
The rose deprived of her fragrant power
Unless three thorns draw drops of one blood
The spider whose web is woven wrong
The fly frightened by her own flight's whir

The half-thoughts, the distances of pain!
An apple stops growing as great as a boulder
The ant on his hind legs reaches to your neck
And all the leaves that have ever fallen
Resurrect a wall around summer's wide bed

The half-thoughts, the distances of pain!
Those chains of memory that drag the mind back
Are not so terrible as the magnet earth
Who sooner or later takes away
Her gifts of yesterday tomorrow and today

The half-thoughts, the distances of pain!
The egg on end at the tip of the breeze
The halt in the middle of a murdering word
The child with eyes in the back of its head
Love in one, a stranger in the other

The half-thoughts, the distances of pain!
The wait before the ear grows back
The leap in the dark, the moving package
The cold hand of water that wanders the warm quarry
The severed treetrunk forgetting the way to crash

The half-thoughts, the distances of pain!
Voluntary grief in the midst of joy
Vines withering as if of their own accord
The shadows thrown, the shadows swallowed
As though their bodies had nothing to do with them

The half-thoughts, the distances of pain!
To know how many days you'll live
Crook your foot to cage the tiger's tears
Oh but the tiger came one day
To lick the fingers that decreed their own fate

The half-thoughts, the distances of pain!
The skeleton is glad his bones are not flesh
But sometimes the lips are webbed as a navel
The navel braver than a questioned skull
Whose days were numbered as the hair of its head

The half-thoughts, the distances of pain!
Decay's unloosing is the tightest token
The tongue shakes hands though it lack four fingers
The word omitted by mistake
Is the unwatched window on the night of escape

The half-thoughts, the distances of pain!
The flowers blooming underground
The underwater sleepers sleeping
Washed ashore, kicking like fishes
Unable to wake or walk in their sleep or swim

The half-thoughts, the distances of pain!
The rat jumping out of a handful of tears

The man found drowned in a horse's track
A rat might despair in a sea of tears
A man could swim in, but not in a handful

The half-thoughts, the distances of pain!
The hour that beats as if the blood
Of all the hours had been pumped through it
Lend me your heart for an hour or so
And the day will forget that it always belonged to you

The half-thoughts, the distances of pain!
How long does it take for you to hear
The bells that ring in my head at your feet
I hear neither toll nor celebration
Because your heart's hour neither begins nor ends

The half-thoughts, the distances of pain!
A body walks through the mirror of self
Leaves the mirror lacerated
The bird groans at the sight of a child
With love in its eyes, death in its smile

The half-thoughts, the distances of pain!
Have you overheard the light grow dim or seen
The dark talking to itself in the dark
If flesh and bone turned one into the other
How could I tell if your bones were flesh and flowing

The half-thoughts, the distances of pain!
The highest tree is not the hardest
The sickest cat is not the most mortal
The reddest berry is not always the sweetest
The cat ate the berry and climbed the tree it couldn't

The half-thoughts, the distances of pain!
The chopped heart no magic hatchet touched
May let ten pieces live apart

Or grow together, more sinewy than ever
The owl growls, the cat-fit's forfeited

The half-thoughts, the distances of pain!
The cat's fit left the old owl doubting
Can two hands hold their own slow crumbling
And if the nose whiff its own body rotting?
Not only the eye may live in its own ruin!

The Fortunes Of Edith Sitwell

I *Footprints in the Sands of Time*

I can remember you, walking on Cape Cod
Wrapped in *mousseline de soie*
Listening for the nightlong call
Of the absent and abstemious muezzin

At times you reach nobly into a pocket
And take out a copy of Mother Goose
The neurasthenic mulatto on the beach
Waits for you to read in an unemotional voice

But instead you turn to the Baron Munchausen
Who offers you a glass of moselle which you refuse
You do take one of those small cakes from an Irish-Italian
    bakery
And, since it is gummy, put it in your purse

To get away you say you've forgotten your mascara
In reality you visit a meteorologist
The talk of light-years is appalling and consoling
But you are too nomadic to be stopped by this

I see you in the Black Forest now
Eating *marrons glacés* and throwing some away
You are thinking of a malignant poem
And of how knock-kneed princesses are

The scene changes to some place non-Egyptian
You weep for a while and look exquisite and vicious
But no one can cheat you; to the top of the mirador
You fly as if leading an insurrection

Here you write down something illegible and profane
And the virulent masses thank you for your pains
There are cheers and curses from the aristocracy
(Some of whom have done time in Alcatraz)

And it all ends when a salesman from Akron
Identifies a coloratura as his illegitimate daughter
By this time if you're not in Bangalore
You'll wish you were in an igloo, or interplanetary

II   *The Dagger That Drew No Blood*

Who is this new arrival on horseback
A lady with an otherworldly air
Someone shrieks when she draws her cloak apart
A smile is on her face, a dagger is in her heart

One nostril quivers as she slowly sheds a glove
One osprey quivers in her modish cap
She knows she's outnumbered and is risking her life
With an opaline hand she withdraws the bloodless knife

A tremor runs through the heterosexual crowd
Hypnotized by her hair that shakes as though wind
Blew it every whichway, but not a breath of air
Stirs the tassels of the saddle on the horse who suddenly

Kneels on one knee as if praying halfheartedly
"*Mademoiselle de Maupin!*" "*Mademoiselle de Maupin!*"
"It is not!" "No, it is not!"
The crowd, though excited as a cult, is divided

Looking coldblooded and hypersensitive
She advances like Lady Macbeth
Now in the center of the circling band
The Aztec stiletto hovers high in her hand

At her feet with lips bleeding from kissing the jeweled
    shoes
Is Pedro, an imbecile, whom no one else knows
No one, except the poetess, who from the turret
Has watched the unfolding of this pathological drama

126

"Stop!" she cries. "Do not slay your half-brother!"
The other, with obstinate incestuous rage
Stabs Pedro three times in his muscular neck
He continues to adore her and does not bleed

"*Fratricida!*" — a jibe from the disgusted people
In the midst of whom the poetess has appeared
She wrests the dagger from the would-be murderess
And thrusts it slowly through the ribs of her own breast

Then mounts on the horse with an otherworldly air
Fratricida, mourning, climbs the stair to the mirador
Leaving Pedro covered with her cape of paillettes
Which the crowd tears to pieces before sterilizing him

III   *The Orphic Mirror*

The open-air morgue of the Colorado Desert
Is searched by the sun from the China Sea
Through white Cordova hides the Crocodile River
But a polar grotto such as Coleridge knew

Has been opened up for you. Oneiric excretions
Prolong the walls into loving landscapes
Where you set foot, the panic-stricken flowers
Breathe calmly as an outlaw riding on Olympus

O, the oboist honks a heartrending rendition
Of Tchaikowsky who knew what it was to go hungry
For love, not for food, and the wheyfaced cobra
Like an *objet-d'art*, expects the next century

To grow hotheaded and appreciate him too
Bah to the infidels, the centipedes are manna
One *peseta* to a slum-child works like hormones
Ordered from the catalogue of props for an opera

I see you in a world no longer cannibalistic
The tears of Niobe which you catch in a poem's cup
When poured out again are words of purest gold
Which float like a halo toward the nearest hero

One day the universe will make you a present
It will be this pearly earth which you always wanted
With a highbrow child like an acrobat atop it
A toe hold on Mont Blanc and whirling through the heavens

For the moment you are resting and looking in a mirror
Remembering the Parisian with whom you crossed the
    Channel
Whose identity you gathered as he gazed towards the Orient
You vanished like Eurydice and found in your hands a harp

Oh the harp we hear is like the nightlong rain
Plucked from the wind as you walked on Cape Cod
The lady in the mirror with an otherworldly air
Shudders and is silent as she combs her singing hair

Ballet For Tamara Toumanova

Tamara on her toes goes through snowflakes,
Large and white as little butterflies
Which never light on the same place twice
And never quite lie down.

Tamara's toes, too, seem to skim the ground
As though the green grass were greenest water,
As if to touch it she would drown.
Yes, the slow grass would turn to quick water
If only to hold Tamara all around!

But a house is being built for her
With tiger-tooth nails and rugs of bees' fur,
The front doorknob is a swarming tear
Wept by a giant the first time he saw
A pirouette! ('Twas Tamara in the snow.)

The sun with tongue of softest gold
Carves the windows in the walls of mist
And windowpanes are tears of joy
Brought by boys who heard Tamara's name
Spoken in their dreams! Ah, Tamara's

Heart gives a leap and leaps with her
To the shimmering door where she knocks and listens.
Although the door is a wide-open rose
(Its doorknob core a great dewdrop)
The rose must close before the door will open . . .

Tamara with her black hair warm as summer honey
Asks a pretty orphan if he will keep her company
Until the roof is ready. Doves and flowers
Scatter plumes and petals on the spiderweb rafters
And fishes hold hands to make a shiny chimney
More wonderful than any in China or India.

But Tamara! Who is that in a hood as black
As your hair, dark hair as sweet as night's honey?

Tamara turns her great green eyes
On his eyes, green too, as only eyes can be

He holds out a key, she holds out her hand,
But the snowflakes, hard as diamond butterflies,
Have stopped in midair, like a net of stars
That no one, not the melancholy man
Nor even Tamara can move among!

The good giant looking for his missing tear
(For giants always save their rare tears)
Passed his hand like a headless beast
With five legs and five sharp teeth
(Somewhere the tear was trembling, waiting.
Someday the tear would shiver with cold.
For tears, like hearts whose sweat they are,
As quick as hearts, may change from hot to cold)
Over the sleeping mountain's armpit,
There where the constellation's prisoners
(Still as the photograph of a dream)
Had lost all hope of ever touching
Hand or lip, skin or hair again!

But warm as a tongue or cool as the shadow
A bee designs on breast or shoulder,
The giant longed for the touch of a tear
He could call his own . . . The tear lay there
In the heart of the rose, then tumbled in his palm
As though the rose shed its first drop of grief.
The butterfly stars cut the giant fingers
But the hand stayed on its back like a beast
While the monster's eyes were fixed on Tamara . . .

Tamara didn't care now, if the door were open,
Reading her future in the crystal tear
On the animal's belly . . . The fish broke the chimney,
Frantic as birds, they whispered, speechless

Warnings in the shells of Tamara's ears;
The orphans awoke and their dream disappeared;
Only the man in the hood was happy.

The twisting key put its head in his pocket,
He shook his cloak and the claws of his feet
Left the ground to find a branch to fit.
Ah, Tamara, your beautiful neck is the tree!

But what she sees is stronger than feeling . . .
Riding a horse on the edge of the world,
The world is flat as fortune's wheel,
The horse's tail is an old man's beard,
Tamara's face is a frozen place
Where two birds live in the ice of her eyes
And the flame of her mouth is colder than the sky.

Tamara! Can't you feel the startled blood
That jewels your breast and makes your skin more white?
But Tamara's eyes, green as hummingbirds,
Plunge their beaks in the tear and beat
Their wings against that other ice.

And her hand, as if hypnotized, has touched
The horse and herself on the edge of the world,
And they fall! — from the edge of the world like a tear
From the world's closing eyelid . . . Tamara, crying,
Fades from the light to follow her image

From the light of day, but the man of night
With wings like hair is taking her away . . .
The giant hurls his tear like a moon
And it bursts like sun around Tamara
As he plucks the black wings from her shoulders.

But where is Tamara? . . .

                              The giant's tears
Make a fountain, now, in his melancholy garden
And he always watches the black statue there
Catching the snow like melting butterflies,
Butterflies melting on her hand and dark hair.

The Net Of Night

i
What survives the risk the day takes
Leaping inside the dark egg of evening?
And how can a man arise and walk
Out of the unveiled egg of the mind
Or lost there for his swift forever
Never leave that land of dreams?

There the summer on its back
Crawls with flowers marvelous as maggots.
There the moon turns ashes in the mouth:
Take but a swallow and the body glows
More than a woman hewn from the eye's rose.

Float, fly with me and we'll see what we see.
Sometimes we believe the unseen the half-seen
Sometimes we are frightened by we know not what
Sometimes we are happy and know not why
And tears fall in the heart from an unseen sky.

There the trees of flesh and blood
Open at a touch and fold you in
All your blood begins to beat
With the tree's blood and your bones
Melt and your only body flows
In and out of the heart of the tree.
When the tree's fruit finally falls
It's hard to choose and no one knows
From which bitten apple you'll jump to scare the eater.

ii
Night turns round the world's one eye
Like death around the image of desire.
Memory's luminous bones awake
To flood the dark with the glow of the grave.
Across the desert that thrives on the known
And known (watered with tears of others and other

Tears that one day you will call your own)
Night is the mysterious beast
We ride upon but never see.

Night is the knock that covers the heart with stones
Night brings the sorrow that makes the day more dear
Night's cloaked woman, eye of moon
Nurses her children who rave in the sun.
O frozen eye of cold cold moon
You melt forever yet never get smaller!

iii
The nut of night under the dream's hammer
Cracks like a heart between love's teeth
Night's fruit open as a heart rolls back —
An eye with its secrets hatched.
How the hazards multiply with feathers
Whether, whether or not half of them
Fly back home like hammers.

In the downcast forest where fishes wander
Where no one anticipates the sky's coming closer
And closer, the heart of the world beating faster
Day making room in the grave for night
Birds of love around the nest of death
Winding like winter in and out the years
Turn with a sorrow that makes the day more dear.

Black as the moon before the new moon's tipped
By a touch of the sun's tongue and spills
Itself into itself, the unopened eye
Is midnight's denizen under the trees
Of luminous bones no wind but memory rattles.

The homeless roses that the statues pick
Melt in their cold hands and the sick lips
Of animals too human, too human to live

Move like the insect-catching hairs
On leaves of the sun dew. Birds bigger
Than father or mother contract their claws
Rise with the moving package, drop it
At your own feet, you've no hands to open it
All but your ankles a-wallow in the box
Broken or unbroken you have no way of knowing.

iv
The black boat with its luminous eye
Glides like a lion through the net of night
A lunar skin like a wrong-wove web
Floats in the dark until a neck is rigged:
If it jib your throat take the skin by the hunch
And fill it with everything warm that you touch!

The black boat with a luminous eye
Lays its head near a star on the edge of day.
The sun may drag it away by the mane
Tonight again the lion's mesh fades like a flame.
Roses in the dark are boneless as your breasts
Roses in the day show your body missing.
I found a hump in the air one night
Never knew to which head all the kisses belonged
For the hump went down before daylight.

My hand is caught in the trap of the tree
And you may not see the eater that mysterious beast.
The unopened package walks away like an egg
The moon's favorite child still stands on its head
The black heart's boat with its luminous eye
Slides like a lion through the net of night
Leaves the boneless statues unable to move a muscle
Their frozen hands flowing with roses. See
The dead plants sweat again. Hear!
How the skinless beast of the day is howling.

135

The Face Of The Earth

Sand tears fall; time's tears always falling
Fall through the mind like words in a poem.
The rollicking beast that knows its own future
Winds a rope from the desert roses,
Luminous bones no wind but memory rattles.

The mind's fingers fondle the world's hot body
And finding the world without legs or arms
Hurl it back in the bed of the void!
And I heard with horror the fatal song:
With no hands and no feet, the world crawls along.

If trees of blood could grow where blood is wasted,
One branch of its festering fruit would stop all wars,
One berry of the branch explode a poison
Blue enough to rot sun, moon and stars —
If trees of blood could grow where blood is wasted.

In sleep's deep pocket the writhing key
With its heart in its throat seeks a door to open,
A window to pitch its humped heart through,
Until a hand like a frozen corpse
Lies down beside it to keep the dream warm.

Lullaby, lullaby, tiger, daughter,
The jungle of the world will take you for its own.
If nothing on the face of the earth stands still,
Nothing on the face of the earth is known;
When you stray from my fable, what will you become?

The dream-machine needs a new driver,
Poet! enemy of peace . . .
The songbird has yet to be understood,
The boundaries of sleep to be explored
And the great dead awake.

Spring, too, fools us all with flowers:
They creep across the earth's sad face

Until it seems to be smiling . . .
Another dawn, another breath to take,
And the mind's mirror searches for a sign of life.

Imagination's under the human microscope!
As far as the eye can straddle,
Be it further than heaven or hell,
Meaningless gestures of farewell
Fill the horizon with the heart's stark hope.

The dark heart's hope is changed to flame
And burns the navel to a skull!
Nor waits until the world's transformed
To another world, this is the world
That cannot stay the same!

Like the voice in the fire when the fire goes out,
It seems you never were
But when the wild winds blow
My soul is covered with a voice like snow
And the seed underneath is what the mute child seeks.

The gnome continues to claim a father
It never knew, and the old man of the sea,
The seer with one eye, passes by in silence;
The woman in the red cloak reappears
And the face at the window speaks:

The half-thoughts, the distances of pain,
Have found their other selves, pain is so near
It needs no perspective to make it seem strange!
John Soul's a beggar, Tom Body's a thief,
And the sooner they know it the better it will be.

Night! night! the last land that will fall.
Honor its exiles now, its martyrs,
And the handful that defend it to the last door,

137

And honor even more
The mighty history of its ruins and visions.

Wonder is the watchword!
The light of day approaches like a sword.
The light of night consumes the unseen air,
Just as a white bird, gliding through noon,
Takes whiteness from the sky and gives the sky its blue.

Farewell, Tamara, bride of my best friend . . .
Now his desire will flow
With flaming tears to make your body glow.
The clouds of happiness drop their rain of horror:
In each foul pool, tomorrow stalks its prey.

Weep if you can, laugh if you must
At all that once was nothing, at everything that's dust.
But for this man, shed no tear:
The world for him is the swarming tear
Of eternity, with no face to forsake.

The heart at the end of the world feeds today
With veins that flow back to time's beginning.
And then, and what more? . . .
The more that's left unsaid, the more there is to say.
Oh the irresponsible dead that life must answer for!

The world's a mirror, to break it is to die.
The way of death is wider than the road to glory.
Man can perish through love alone.
But the wine of glory without the bread of love
Turns the tongue to stone.

The rope, the plank, the poem,
Love, life, glory, call it what you will,
Draws to a close and gives you a chilly feeling.
"The clouds are looking for the wind!"
They are going, and the children are going.

Envoi and farewell . . .
Perhaps we'll meet in hell or heaven.
And there'll be other eyes to open
And see what else there is to see
On the face of the earth that once belonged to me.

*Printed March 1972 in Santa Barbara for the
Black Sparrow Press by Noel Young. Design by
Barbara Martin. This edition is limited to
1000 copies in paper wrappers; 200 hardcover
copies numbered & signed by the poet; & 26
lettered copies handbound in boards by Earle
Gray signed & each with an original collage by
Charles Henri Ford.*

CHARLES HENRI FORD was born in Mississippi. Before he was twenty he had published his poetry in a dozen literary magazines, and was editing one of his own, *Blues: A Magazine of New Rhythms* (1929-1931). His first book, *The Garden of Disorder* (1938), is a collection of poems to which William Carlos Williams contributed an introduction. *The Overturned Lake* (1941) continued his experiments in surrealism in the lyric form. *Sleep In A Nest of Flames* (1949) includes a foreword by Edith Sitwell and fresh experiments — ballads, epigrams, nursery rhymes among them. From that time on, his work led to a new lyricism and to new material, prose-poems, found-poetry, and finally to collage or poster-poems, *Spare Parts* (1966) and *Silver Flower Coo* (1968).

During the second world war, Ford edited the highly influential Surrealist magazine *View* (1940-1947), where a number of young American poets were first published. He also turned his talents to painting and photography, and had exhibitions in London, Paris and New York. In the mid-sixties he dedicated himself to film making. His first full-length feature, *Johnny Minotaur*, was released in 1971 to praise from avant-garde film critics.

Charles Henri Ford lives and works in New York City and Crete.